This book belongs to:

....

TREASURED RECIPES

your favorite recipe journal and organizer

ROCKRIDGE PRESS

How to Use this Recipe Book

There is perhaps no better or more touching metaphor for life than a blank recipe book. What starts out as bare will transform over time into a rich and varied collection built upon shared memories and experiences. These pages are here to help you tell your own personal story of food, family, and friendship.

This is a customizable recipe book. You will not find predetermined recipe sections of breakfasts, appetizers, main dishes, and so on. You get to choose the food categories that you want to include. The book provides you with color-coded organization so that no matter the recipe classifications you decide upon, you can easily find the section you're looking for by color. For example, the first recipe section is color-coded orange. When you go to page 17, you'll see a recipe design that highlights orange throughout the section.

The table of contents on the following pages lets you create a recipe journal that works for you. You'll fill in both the recipe sections and the recipe titles. Some people love to entertain and will want to document their best appetizer and cocktail recipes. Others might never host but are eager to have their recipes for favorite holiday meals, slow cooker dishes, and pastas in one place. You may want to begin by reviewing the recipes you already know you want to write down to help you choose your sections. This cookbook has eight recipe sections. In each section there are 15 recipe pages, allowing you to document a total of 120 recipes. Once you've chosen a section, you can start writing down recipe titles. The page numbers are already noted, so make sure that the page number listed for your recipe title in the table of contents matches the page you write the recipe on. On the opposite page are examples of what you might do to customize your table of contents.

The template for each recipe allows you to write down a title, the source of the recipe, the number of people it serves, prep time, cook time, notes, ingredients, and cooking instructions. Use the notes to record memories of the recipe, detail adaptations, list a holiday it's perfect for, highlight another recipe to pair it with, and so on. It's up to you! This book was designed to give you plenty of space to write recipe ingredients and instructions, in particular. If you run out of recipe pages, download and print more from CallistoMediaBooks.com/TreasuredRecipes.

SECTION: *Breakfast* **16**

Aunt Tina's Pancakes 17

Stuffed French Toast 18

Bacon-and-Egg Casserole 19

20

21

SECTION: *Sides* **32**

Green Beans with Slivered Almonds 33

Roasted Broccoli 34

35

Contents

SECTION:

16

17

18

19

20

21

22

23

24

25

26

27

28

29

30

31

SECTION: **32**

33

34

35

36

37

38

39

40

41

42

43

44

45

46

47

SECTION:

48

49

50

51

52

53

54

55

56

57

58

59

60

61

62

63

SECTION: **64**

65

66

67

68

69

70

71

72

73

74

75

76

77

78

79

SECTION: 80

81

82

83

84

85

86

87

88

89

90

91

92

93

94

95

SECTION:

96

97

98

99

100

101

102

103

104

105

106

107

108

109

110

111

SECTION: 112

113

114

115

116

117

118

119

120

121

122

123

124

125

126

127

SECTION: 128

129

130

131

132

133

134

135

136

137

138

139

140

141

142

143

SECTION:
The people who give you their food give you their heart.
CESAR CHAVEZ

Recipe title: *From:*

SERVES:

PREP TIME:

COOK TIME:

NOTES

INGREDIENTS

INSTRUCTIONS

Recipe title:

From:

SERVES:

PREP TIME:

COOK TIME:

NOTES

INGREDIENTS

INSTRUCTIONS

Recipe title: *From:*

SERVES:

PREP TIME:

COOK TIME:

NOTES

INGREDIENTS

INSTRUCTIONS

Recipe title:

From:

NOTES

SERVES:

PREP TIME:

COOK TIME:

INGREDIENTS

INSTRUCTIONS

Recipe title:

From:

SERVES:

PREP TIME:

COOK TIME:

NOTES

INGREDIENTS

INSTRUCTIONS

Recipe title:

From:

SERVES:

PREP TIME:

COOK TIME:

NOTES

INGREDIENTS

INSTRUCTIONS

Recipe title: *From:*

SERVES:

PREP TIME:

COOK TIME:

NOTES

INGREDIENTS

INSTRUCTIONS

Recipe title:

From:

SERVES:

PREP TIME:

COOK TIME:

NOTES

INGREDIENTS

INSTRUCTIONS

Recipe title: *From:*

SERVES:

PREP TIME:

COOK TIME:

NOTES

INGREDIENTS

INSTRUCTIONS

NOTES

INGREDIENTS

INSTRUCTIONS

Recipe title:

From:

SERVES:

PREP TIME:

COOK TIME:

Recipe title: *From:*

SERVES:

PREP TIME:

COOK TIME:

NOTES

INGREDIENTS

INSTRUCTIONS

Recipe title:

From:

SERVES:

PREP TIME:

COOK TIME:

NOTES

INGREDIENTS

INSTRUCTIONS

Recipe title: *From:*

SERVES:

PREP TIME:

COOK TIME:

NOTES

INGREDIENTS

INSTRUCTIONS

Recipe title:

From:

SERVES:

PREP TIME:

COOK TIME:

NOTES

INGREDIENTS

INSTRUCTIONS

Recipe title: *From:*

SERVES:

PREP TIME:

COOK TIME:

NOTES

INGREDIENTS

INSTRUCTIONS

SECTION:
Always read the entire recipe first.
APRIL BLOOMFIELD

Recipe title: *From:*

SERVES:

PREP TIME:

COOK TIME:

NOTES

INGREDIENTS

INSTRUCTIONS

Recipe title:

From:

SERVES:

PREP TIME:

COOK TIME:

NOTES

INGREDIENTS

INSTRUCTIONS

Recipe title: *From:*

SERVES:

PREP TIME:

COOK TIME:

NOTES

INGREDIENTS

INSTRUCTIONS

Recipe title:

From:

SERVES:

PREP TIME:

COOK TIME:

NOTES

INGREDIENTS

INSTRUCTIONS

Recipe title: *From:*

SERVES:

PREP TIME:

COOK TIME:

NOTES

INGREDIENTS

INSTRUCTIONS

Recipe title:

From:

NOTES

SERVES:

PREP TIME:

COOK TIME:

INGREDIENTS

INSTRUCTIONS

Recipe title: *From:*

SERVES:

PREP TIME:

COOK TIME:

NOTES

INGREDIENTS

INSTRUCTIONS

Recipe title:

From:

SERVES:

PREP TIME:

COOK TIME:

NOTES

INGREDIENTS

INSTRUCTIONS

Recipe title: *From:*

SERVES:

PREP TIME:

COOK TIME:

NOTES

INGREDIENTS

INSTRUCTIONS

Recipe title:

From:

SERVES:

PREP TIME:

COOK TIME:

NOTES

INGREDIENTS

INSTRUCTIONS

Recipe title: *From:*

SERVES:

PREP TIME:

COOK TIME:

NOTES

INGREDIENTS

INSTRUCTIONS

Recipe title:

From:

SERVES:

PREP TIME:

COOK TIME:

NOTES

INGREDIENTS

INSTRUCTIONS

Recipe title: *From:*

SERVES:

PREP TIME:

COOK TIME:

NOTES

INGREDIENTS

INSTRUCTIONS

Recipe title:

From:

SERVES:

PREP TIME:

COOK TIME:

NOTES

INGREDIENTS

INSTRUCTIONS

Recipe title: *From:*

SERVES:

PREP TIME:

COOK TIME:

NOTES

INGREDIENTS

INSTRUCTIONS

SECTION:

The only reward for anything is food.

TINA FEY

Recipe title: *From:*

SERVES:

PREP TIME:

COOK TIME:

NOTES

INGREDIENTS

INSTRUCTIONS

Recipe title:

From:

SERVES:

PREP TIME:

COOK TIME:

NOTES

INGREDIENTS

INSTRUCTIONS

Recipe title: *From:*

SERVES:

PREP TIME:

COOK TIME:

NOTES

INGREDIENTS

INSTRUCTIONS

Recipe title:

From:

SERVES:

PREP TIME:

COOK TIME:

NOTES

INGREDIENTS

INSTRUCTIONS

Recipe title: *From:*

SERVES:

PREP TIME:

COOK TIME:

NOTES

INGREDIENTS

INSTRUCTIONS

Recipe title:

From:

SERVES:

PREP TIME:

COOK TIME:

NOTES

INGREDIENTS

INSTRUCTIONS

Recipe title: *From:*

SERVES:

PREP TIME:

COOK TIME:

NOTES

INGREDIENTS

INSTRUCTIONS

Recipe title:

From:

SERVES:

PREP TIME:

COOK TIME:

NOTES

INGREDIENTS

INSTRUCTIONS

Recipe title:

From:

SERVES:

PREP TIME:

COOK TIME:

NOTES

INGREDIENTS

INSTRUCTIONS

Recipe title:

From:

SERVES:

PREP TIME:

COOK TIME:

NOTES

INGREDIENTS

INSTRUCTIONS

Recipe title: *From:*

SERVES:

PREP TIME:

COOK TIME:

NOTES

INGREDIENTS

INSTRUCTIONS

Recipe title:

From:

SERVES:

PREP TIME:

COOK TIME:

NOTES

INGREDIENTS

INSTRUCTIONS

Recipe title: *From:*

SERVES:

PREP TIME:

COOK TIME:

NOTES

INGREDIENTS

INSTRUCTIONS

Recipe title:

From:

SERVES:

PREP TIME:

COOK TIME:

NOTES

INGREDIENTS

INSTRUCTIONS

Recipe title:

From:

SERVES:

PREP TIME:

COOK TIME:

NOTES

INGREDIENTS

INSTRUCTIONS

SECTION:
If you're afraid of butter, use cream.
JULIA CHILD

Recipe title:

From:

SERVES:

PREP TIME:

COOK TIME:

NOTES

INGREDIENTS

INSTRUCTIONS

Recipe title:

From:

SERVES:

PREP TIME:

COOK TIME:

NOTES

INGREDIENTS

INSTRUCTIONS

Recipe title:

From:

SERVES:

PREP TIME:

COOK TIME:

NOTES

INGREDIENTS

INSTRUCTIONS

Recipe title:

From:

SERVES:

PREP TIME:

COOK TIME:

NOTES

INGREDIENTS

INSTRUCTIONS

Recipe title: *From:*

SERVES:

PREP TIME:

COOK TIME:

NOTES

INGREDIENTS

INSTRUCTIONS

Recipe title:

From:

SERVES:

PREP TIME:

COOK TIME:

NOTES

INGREDIENTS

INSTRUCTIONS

Recipe title:

From:

SERVES:

PREP TIME:

COOK TIME:

NOTES

INGREDIENTS

INSTRUCTIONS

Recipe title:

From:

SERVES:

PREP TIME:

COOK TIME:

NOTES

INGREDIENTS

INSTRUCTIONS

Recipe title: *From:*

SERVES:

PREP TIME:

COOK TIME:

NOTES

INGREDIENTS

INSTRUCTIONS

Recipe title:

From:

NOTES

SERVES:

PREP TIME:

COOK TIME:

INGREDIENTS

INSTRUCTIONS

Recipe title:

From:

SERVES:

PREP TIME:

COOK TIME:

NOTES

INGREDIENTS

INSTRUCTIONS

Recipe title:

From:

SERVES:

PREP TIME:

COOK TIME:

NOTES

INGREDIENTS

INSTRUCTIONS

Recipe title:

From:

SERVES:

PREP TIME:

COOK TIME:

NOTES

INGREDIENTS

INSTRUCTIONS

Recipe title:

From:

SERVES:

PREP TIME:

COOK TIME:

NOTES

INGREDIENTS

INSTRUCTIONS

Recipe title:

From:

SERVES:

PREP TIME:

COOK TIME:

NOTES

INGREDIENTS

INSTRUCTIONS

SECTION:

There is no such thing as a little garlic.

ARTHUR BAER

Recipe title:

From:

SERVES:

PREP TIME:

COOK TIME:

NOTES

INGREDIENTS

INSTRUCTIONS

Recipe title:

From:

NOTES

SERVES:

PREP TIME:

COOK TIME:

INGREDIENTS

INSTRUCTIONS

Recipe title:

From:

SERVES:

PREP TIME:

COOK TIME:

NOTES

INGREDIENTS

INSTRUCTIONS

Recipe title:

From:

SERVES:

PREP TIME:

COOK TIME:

NOTES

INGREDIENTS

INSTRUCTIONS

Recipe title: *From:*

SERVES:

PREP TIME:

COOK TIME:

NOTES

INGREDIENTS

INSTRUCTIONS

Recipe title:

From:

SERVES:

PREP TIME:

COOK TIME:

NOTES

INGREDIENTS

INSTRUCTIONS

Recipe title:

From:

SERVES:

PREP TIME:

COOK TIME:

NOTES

INGREDIENTS

INSTRUCTIONS

Recipe title:

From:

NOTES

SERVES:

PREP TIME:

COOK TIME:

INGREDIENTS

INSTRUCTIONS

Recipe title: *From:*

SERVES:

PREP TIME:

COOK TIME:

NOTES

INGREDIENTS

INSTRUCTIONS

Recipe title:

From:

SERVES:

PREP TIME:

COOK TIME:

NOTES

INGREDIENTS

INSTRUCTIONS

Recipe title:

From:

SERVES:

PREP TIME:

COOK TIME:

NOTES

INGREDIENTS

INSTRUCTIONS

Recipe title:

From:

SERVES:

PREP TIME:

COOK TIME:

NOTES

INGREDIENTS

INSTRUCTIONS

Recipe title: *From:*

SERVES:

PREP TIME:

COOK TIME:

NOTES

INGREDIENTS

INSTRUCTIONS

Recipe title:

From:

SERVES:

PREP TIME:

COOK TIME:

NOTES

INGREDIENTS

INSTRUCTIONS

Recipe title:

From:

SERVES:

PREP TIME:

COOK TIME:

NOTES

INGREDIENTS

INSTRUCTIONS

SECTION:

Cooking is honest work

DAVID CHANG

Recipe title: From:

SERVES:

PREP TIME:

COOK TIME:

NOTES

INGREDIENTS

INSTRUCTIONS

Recipe title:

From:

NOTES

SERVES:

PREP TIME:

COOK TIME:

INGREDIENTS

INSTRUCTIONS

Recipe title: *From:*

SERVES:

PREP TIME:

COOK TIME:

NOTES

INGREDIENTS

INSTRUCTIONS

Recipe title:

From:

NOTES

SERVES:

PREP TIME:

COOK TIME:

INGREDIENTS

INSTRUCTIONS

Recipe title: *From:*

SERVES:

PREP TIME:

COOK TIME:

NOTES

INGREDIENTS

INSTRUCTIONS

Recipe title:

From:

SERVES:

PREP TIME:

COOK TIME:

NOTES

INGREDIENTS

INSTRUCTIONS

Recipe title: *From:*

SERVES:

PREP TIME:

COOK TIME:

NOTES

INGREDIENTS

INSTRUCTIONS

Recipe title:

From:

SERVES:

PREP TIME:

COOK TIME:

NOTES

INGREDIENTS

INSTRUCTIONS

Recipe title: *From:*

SERVES:

PREP TIME:

COOK TIME:

NOTES

INGREDIENTS

INSTRUCTIONS

Recipe title:

From:

SERVES:

PREP TIME:

COOK TIME:

NOTES

INGREDIENTS

INSTRUCTIONS

Recipe title: *From:*

SERVES:

PREP TIME:

COOK TIME:

NOTES

INGREDIENTS

INSTRUCTIONS

Recipe title:

From:

SERVES:

PREP TIME:

COOK TIME:

NOTES

INGREDIENTS

INSTRUCTIONS

Recipe title:

From:

SERVES:

PREP TIME:

COOK TIME:

NOTES

INGREDIENTS

INSTRUCTIONS

Recipe title:

From:

SERVES:

PREP TIME:

COOK TIME:

NOTES

INGREDIENTS

INSTRUCTIONS

Recipe title:

From:

SERVES:

PREP TIME:

COOK TIME:

NOTES

INGREDIENTS

INSTRUCTIONS

SECTION:

First we eat. Then we do everything else.

M.F.K. FISHER

Recipe title:

From:

SERVES:

PREP TIME:

COOK TIME:

NOTES

INGREDIENTS

INSTRUCTIONS

Recipe title:

From:

SERVES:

PREP TIME:

COOK TIME:

NOTES

INGREDIENTS

INSTRUCTIONS

Recipe title: *From:*

SERVES:

PREP TIME:

COOK TIME:

NOTES

INGREDIENTS

INSTRUCTIONS

Recipe title:

From:

SERVES:

PREP TIME:

COOK TIME:

NOTES

INGREDIENTS

INSTRUCTIONS

Recipe title: *From:*

SERVES:

PREP TIME:

COOK TIME:

NOTES

INGREDIENTS

INSTRUCTIONS

NOTES

INGREDIENTS

INSTRUCTIONS

Recipe title:

From:

SERVES:

PREP TIME:

COOK TIME:

Recipe title: *From:*

SERVES:

PREP TIME:

COOK TIME:

NOTES

INGREDIENTS

INSTRUCTIONS

Recipe title:

From:

SERVES:

PREP TIME:

COOK TIME:

NOTES

INGREDIENTS

INSTRUCTIONS

Recipe title: *From:*

SERVES:

PREP TIME:

COOK TIME:

NOTES

INGREDIENTS

INSTRUCTIONS

Recipe title:

From:

SERVES:

PREP TIME:

COOK TIME:

NOTES

INGREDIENTS

INSTRUCTIONS

Recipe title: From:

SERVES:

PREP TIME:

COOK TIME:

NOTES

INGREDIENTS

INSTRUCTIONS

Recipe title:

From:

SERVES:

PREP TIME:

COOK TIME:

NOTES

INGREDIENTS

INSTRUCTIONS

Recipe title: *From:*

SERVES:

PREP TIME:

COOK TIME:

NOTES

INGREDIENTS

INSTRUCTIONS

Recipe title:

From:

NOTES

SERVES:

PREP TIME:

COOK TIME:

INGREDIENTS

INSTRUCTIONS

Recipe title: *From:*

SERVES:

PREP TIME:

COOK TIME:

NOTES

INGREDIENTS

INSTRUCTIONS

SECTION:

A person cooking is a person giving. Even the simplest food is a gift.

LAURIE COLWIN

Recipe title:

From:

SERVES:

PREP TIME:

COOK TIME:

NOTES

INGREDIENTS

INSTRUCTIONS

Recipe title:

From:

SERVES:

PREP TIME:

COOK TIME:

NOTES

INGREDIENTS

INSTRUCTIONS

Recipe title: *From:*

SERVES:

PREP TIME:

COOK TIME:

NOTES

INGREDIENTS

INSTRUCTIONS

Recipe title:

From:

SERVES:

PREP TIME:

COOK TIME:

NOTES

INGREDIENTS

INSTRUCTIONS

Recipe title: *From:*

SERVES:

PREP TIME:

COOK TIME:

NOTES

INGREDIENTS

INSTRUCTIONS

Recipe title:

From:

NOTES

SERVES:

PREP TIME:

COOK TIME:

INGREDIENTS

INSTRUCTIONS

Recipe title: *From:*

SERVES:

PREP TIME:

COOK TIME:

NOTES

INGREDIENTS

INSTRUCTIONS

Recipe title:

From:

SERVES:

PREP TIME:

COOK TIME:

NOTES

INGREDIENTS

INSTRUCTIONS

Recipe title: *From:*

SERVES:

PREP TIME:

COOK TIME:

NOTES

INGREDIENTS

INSTRUCTIONS

Recipe title:

From:

SERVES:

PREP TIME:

COOK TIME:

NOTES

INGREDIENTS

INSTRUCTIONS

Recipe title: *From:*

SERVES:

PREP TIME:

COOK TIME:

NOTES

INGREDIENTS

INSTRUCTIONS

Recipe title:

From:

SERVES:

PREP TIME:

COOK TIME:

NOTES

INGREDIENTS

INSTRUCTIONS

Recipe title: *From:*

SERVES:

PREP TIME:

COOK TIME:

NOTES

INGREDIENTS

INSTRUCTIONS

Recipe title:

From:

SERVES:

PREP TIME:

COOK TIME:

NOTES

INGREDIENTS

INSTRUCTIONS

Recipe title: *From:*

SERVES:

PREP TIME:

COOK TIME:

NOTES

INGREDIENTS

INSTRUCTIONS

Glossary of Cooking Terms

AL DENTE: In pasta cooking, the point where the pasta is just tender with a slightly firm center.

BASTE: To brush melted butter, oil, a marinade, or other liquid over food as it cooks.

BLANCH: To cook vegetables very briefly in boiling water, used primarily to brighten color and soften rather than completely cook the food.

CUBE: To cut into small even pieces, usually about 1 inch on a side for meat, smaller for vegetables. Also, to mechanically tenderize meat by lacerating and pressing (e.g., cubed steak).

DASH: A small amount, usually of a liquid (several drops up to ⅛ teaspoon).

DEGLAZE: To add liquid, often alcohol or broth or a combination, to a hot pan after browning foods, scraping up the cooked bits of food off the surface of the pan.

DICE: To chop into small pieces (smaller than cubes, but larger than minced).

DIVIDED: In ingredient lists, this term indicates that an ingredient is used in two or more steps. The instructions will tell you how much to use when.

DREDGE: To cover with a thin, even coat of flour or breadcrumbs before frying.

FLAKE: To separate into small shreds, as for cooked fish.

FOLD: To blend delicate ingredients such as whipped cream or beaten egg whites gently into a heavier mixture.

GARNISH: Small amounts of foods, often herbs, spices, nuts, or grated cheese, sprinkled over the top of a dish right before serving, as a sensory accent.

JULIENNE: To cut into thin even strips, generally used with vegetables and fruits.

MARINATE: To soak foods in a flavorful liquid that often includes acid, oil, spices, and herbs.

MINCE: To finely chop, usually herbs, garlic, or ginger.

PARBOIL: To partially cook in boiling liquid.

PINCH: A very small amount of salt or spice, literally the amount you can pinch between the thumb and forefinger.

POACH: To cook very gently in hot liquid kept well below the boiling point.

REDUCE: To boil sauce and evaporate some of the water in order to concentrate the flavor or thicken the sauce.

RENDER: To extract animal fat from meat by heating it slowly so that it melts out of the meat.

SAUTÉ: To fry pieces of food in a small amount of fat or oil, moving them often as they cook; sometimes erroneously used as a synonym for "fry."

SCANT: In measuring ingredients, an indication to use barely the amount specified or even slightly less (e.g., a scant cup flour).

SCORE: To make shallow cuts in the surface of certain foods, such as meat or fish.

SEAR: To brown the surface, usually of meat or fish.

SIMMER: To bring a liquid just below or to the boiling point; to cook food in simmering liquid.

STEAM: To cook foods over, but not touching, boiling liquid in a closed pot.

WHIP: To beat ingredients vigorously, specifically in order to incorporate air into the mixture.

ZEST: To remove the colored part of the rind from citrus fruit.

Common Ingredient Substitutions

INGREDIENT	AMOUNT	SUBSTITUTION
Baking powder	1 teaspoon	¼ teaspoon of baking soda mixed with ½ teaspoon cream of tartar
Buttermilk	1 cup	1 cup plain yogurt (not Greek style) or 1 cup milk + 1 tablespoon lemon juice
Chives, minced	1 tablespoon	1 tablespoon scallion greens, minced
Cream (heavy)	1 cup	⅔ cup whole milk + ⅓ cup butter
Crème fraiche	½ cup	⅓ cup sour cream + 2 tablespoons cream
Garlic	1 clove (small)	⅛ teaspoon garlic powder
Ginger (fresh)	1 tablespoon grated	½ teaspoon dried ginger
Herbs, fresh	1 tablespoon	½ to 1 teaspoon dried
Lemon or lime juice	2 teaspoons	1 teaspoon white wine vinegar
Lemon zest	½ teaspoon	1–2 drops lemon extract or lemon oil
Mustard (dried)	½ teaspoon	2 teaspoons Dijon-style mustard

INGREDIENT	AMOUNT	SUBSTITUTION
Mustard (prepared)	1 tablespoon	½ teaspoon dried mustard + 2 teaspoons vinegar + ½ teaspoon water
Oil	1 cup	1 cup applesauce (for baking only)
Red pepper flakes	1 teaspoon	½ teaspoon cayenne or 2–3 dashes Tabasco
Self-rising flour	1 cup	1 cup all-purpose flour + ⅛ teaspoon salt + 1½ teaspoons baking powder
Shallot	1 medium	2 tablespoons diced red onion soaked in water for 5 minutes and drained
Sherry (dry)	½ cup	⅓ cup dry white wine + 2 tablespoons brandy
Sour cream	1 cup	1 cup Greek style plain yogurt
Tomato, fresh	1 large	½ to ⅔ cup drained diced canned tomatoes
Tomato sauce	1 cup	⅓ cup tomato paste + ⅔ cup water

Measurements and Conversions

Volume Equivalents (Liquid)

US STANDARD	US STANDARD	METRIC*
2 tablespoons	1 fl. oz.	30 mL
¼ cup	2 fl. oz.	60 mL
½ cup	4 fl. oz.	120 mL
1 cup	8 fl. oz.	240 mL
1½ cups	12 fl. oz.	355 mL
2 cups or 1 pint	16 fl. oz.	475 mL
4 cups or 1 quart	32 fl. oz.	1 L
1 gallon or 4 quarts	128 fl. oz.	4 L

Volume Equivalents (Dry)

US STANDARD	US STANDARD	METRIC*
⅟₁₆ teaspoon	dash	
⅛ teaspoon	pinch	0.5 mL
3 teaspoons	1 tablespoon	15 mL
⅛ cup	2 tablespoons	30 mL
¼ cup	4 tablespoons	59 mL
⅓ cup	5 tablespoons plus 1 teaspoon	79 mL
½ cup	8 tablespoons	118 mL
¾ cup	12 tablespoons	177 mL
1 cup	16 tablespoons	235 mL
2 cups	1 pint	475 mL
1 pound	16 ounces	455 g

Oven Temperatures

FAHRENHEIT (F)	CELSIUS (C)*
250°F	120°C
300°F	150°C
325°F	165°C
350°F	180°C
375°F	190°C
400°F	200°C
425°F	220°C
450°F	230°C

Weight Equivalents

US STANDARD	METRIC*
½ ounce	15 g
1 ounce	30 g
2 ounces	60 g
4 ounces	115 g
8 ounces	225 g
12 ounces	340 g
16 ounces or 1 pound	455 g

** Metric measurements are approximate*

For general information on our other products and services or to obtain technical support, please contact our Customer Care Department within the U.S. at (866) 744-2665, or outside the U.S. at (510) 253-0500.

Rockridge Press publishes its books in a variety of electronic and print formats. Some content that appears in print may not be available in electronic books, and vice versa.

Print ISBN: 978-1-939754-95-0

Run of out of recipe pages? Download and print the recipe template!
CallistoMediaBooks.com/TreasuredRecipes